Contents

Say the Sounds	4
Tricky Words	5
Spot the Story Setting	6
The Rocket	7
Monsters	17
The Pond	27
Helping	37
The Wind and the Sun	47
Book Week	57
Book Review	68
Character Review	70

This book belongs to

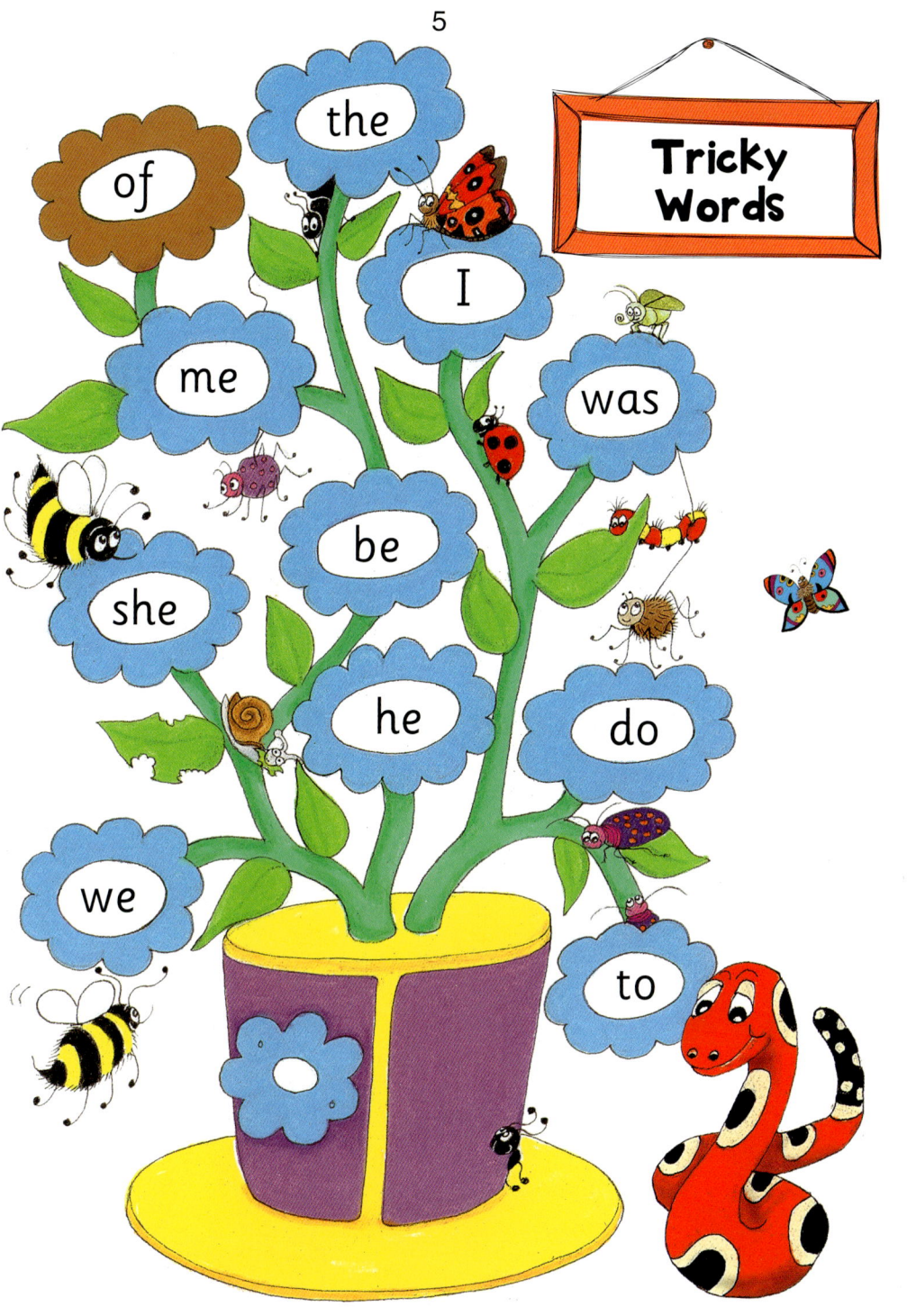

The Rocket

I wish I had a rocket...

to zoom up to the clouds

and jet around the stars a bit...

and land on Planet Mars,

then orbit
around the sun...

until it got too hot

and swoop back on a comet's tail...

...for a picnic

on the moon!

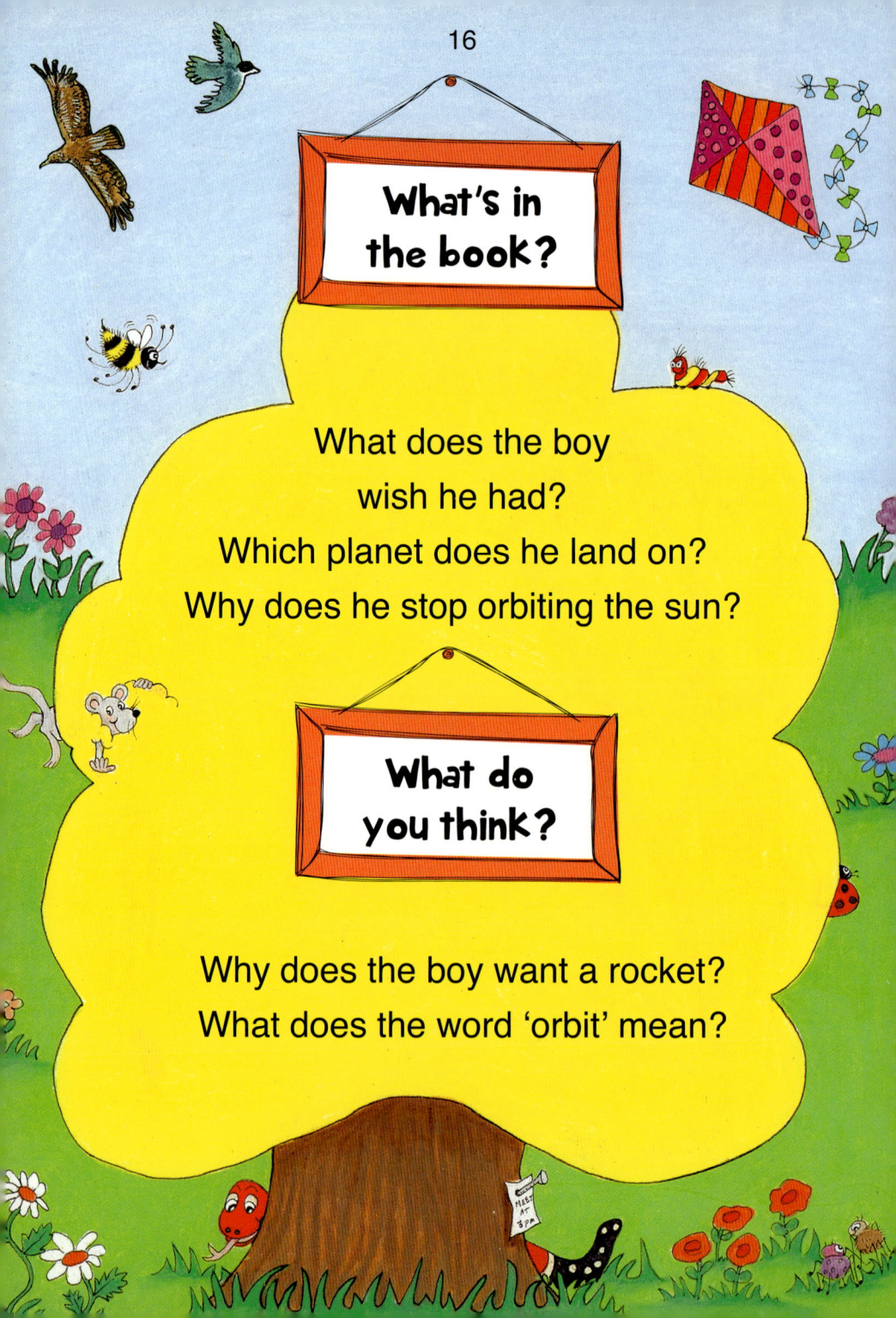

What's in the book?

What does the boy wish he had?
Which planet does he land on?
Why does he stop orbiting the sun?

What do you think?

Why does the boy want a rocket?
What does the word 'orbit' mean?

Monsters

Monsters!

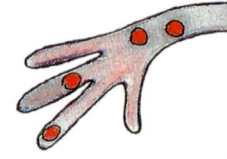

Monsters!

Monsters!

Monsters stomp

and stamp.

Monsters bash

and crash.

Monsters flap

and clap.

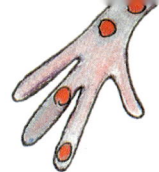

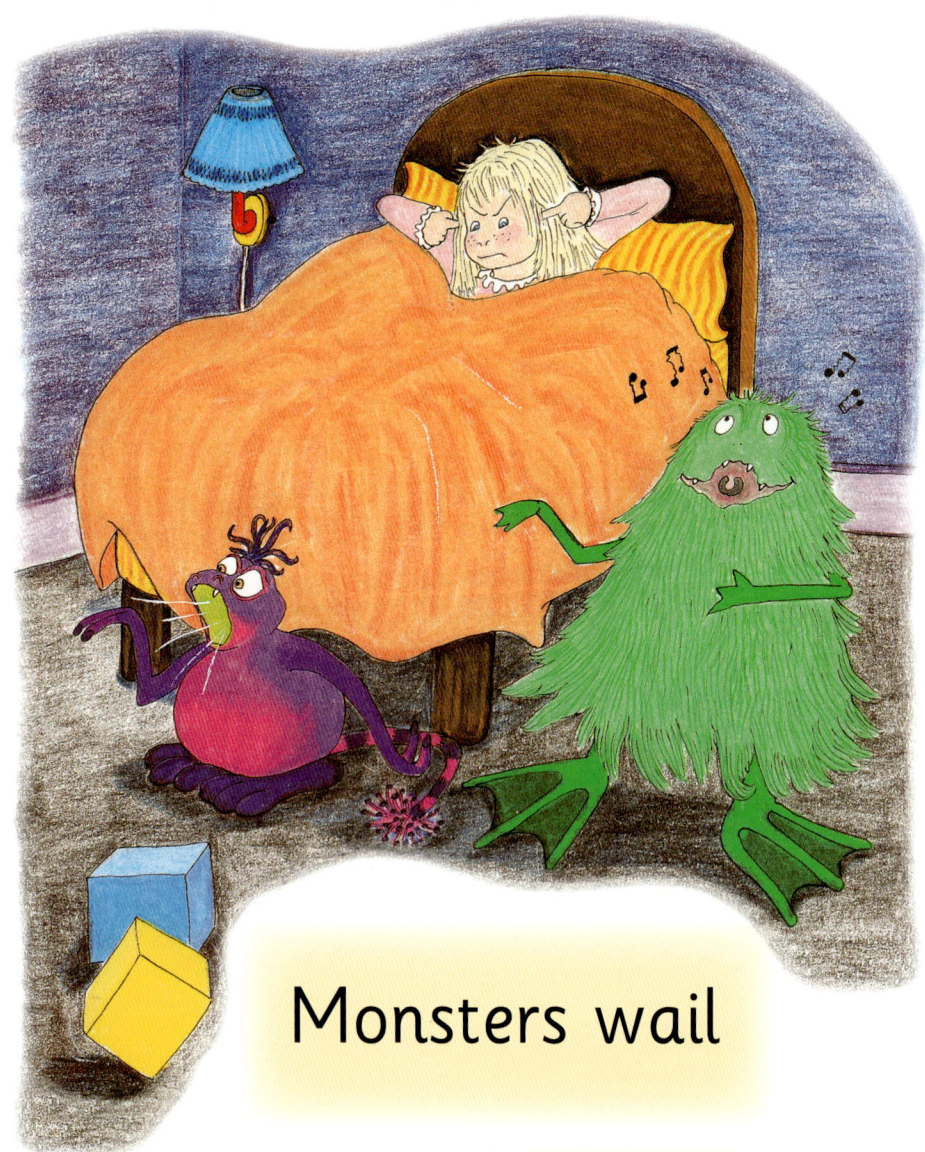

Monsters wail

and shout.

Monsters bang and clang.

Monsters

hop, then stop!

Monsters are sleeping.

Sh!

What's in the book?

What do the monsters stomp and stamp with?
What do the monsters use to bash and crash?
What do the monsters do after they hop?

What do you think?

What do the monsters like doing?
Why is the girl angry with the monsters?

The Pond

Ten ducks.

Ten ducks swim on a big pond.

A big green frog.

The big green frog

sits on a log.

Then the frog

jumps
into
the
pond.

He lands with a loud

splosh!

The ten ducks flap off...

...and the frog has the big pond to himself.

What's in the book?

How many ducks are on the pond?
What is the frog sitting on?
Where does the frog jump?

What do you think?

Why do the ducks all fly away?
Does the frog like having the pond to himself?

Helping

We are helping.

This is Bill, Hinda and me.

We are selling tickets.

This is me. I can jump.

This is Anna.

She paints well.

This is Ben.

CAKE SALE

He is a good cook.

This is Meg.

She is good at kicking.

This is Seth.

He is a good goalkeeper...

...but Meg is a winner!

What's in the book?

What is Anna good at?
What is Ben good at?
Who is a good goalkeeper?

What do you think?

What are the children helping with?
Why is Meg a winner?

The Wind and the Sun

The Wind and the Sun argued.

"I am the strongest!"

shouted the Wind.

"I am!"

glinted the Sun.

"I bet I can get that man's coat off!"

boasted the Wind.

He tried hard,

but the man just shivered and held on to his coat.

"I can do better,"
flashed the Sun.

It got hotter and hotter until the man took off his coat.

The Wind stormed off and the Sun just glittered.

What's in the book?

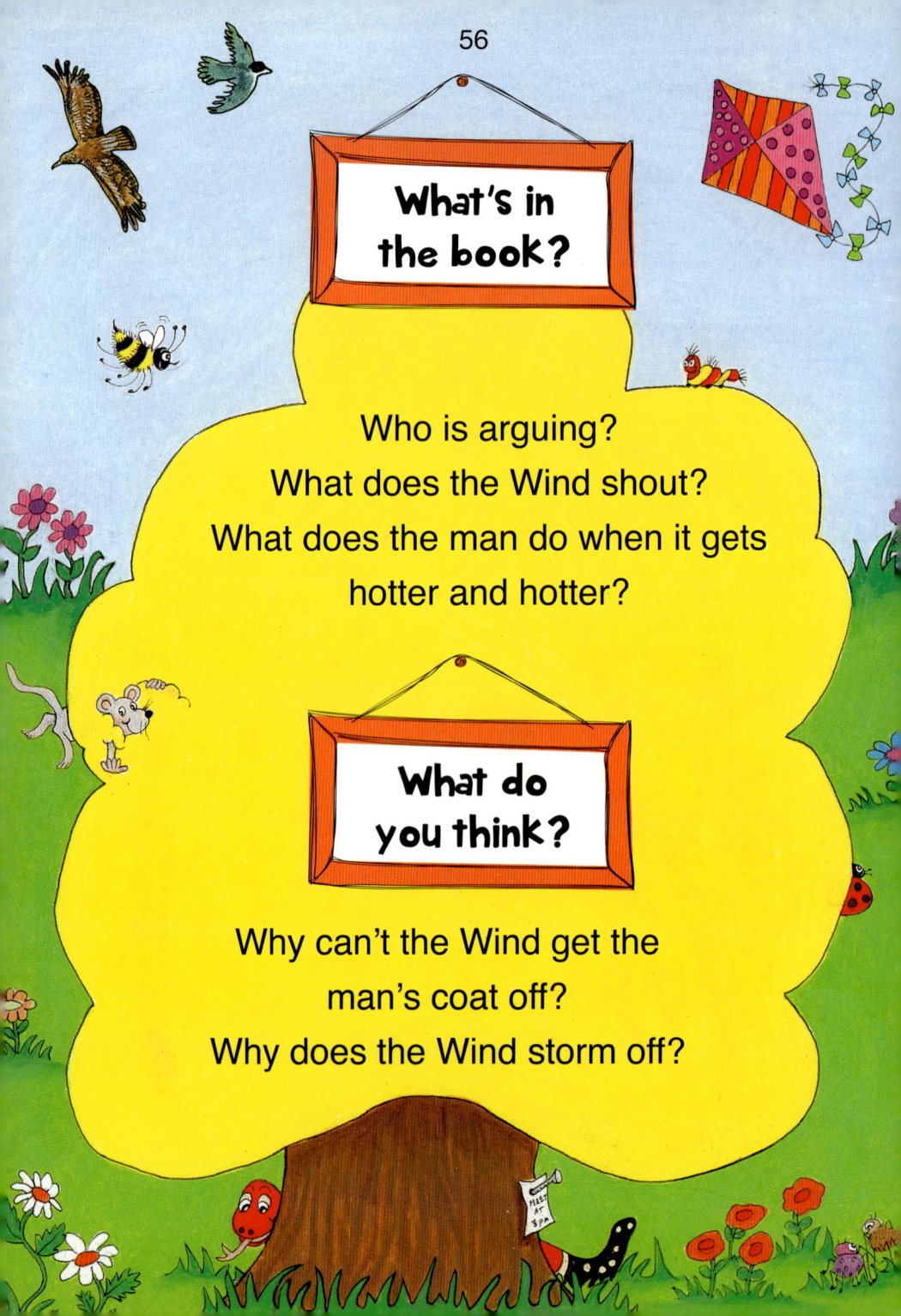

Who is arguing?
What does the Wind shout?
What does the man do when it gets hotter and hotter?

What do you think?

Why can't the Wind get the man's coat off?
Why does the Wind storm off?

Book Week

It was the end of Book Week.

Gus had to dress up as a person from a book.

Adam was Jack

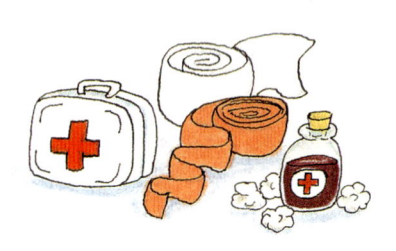

and Kim was Jill.

Jack   Jill

Hinda was Miss Muffet

and Seth was Robin Hood.

Miss Muffet

Robin Hood

Rob was a wizard

and Gus

was...

...a dragon!

What's in the book?

Who is Jack?
Who does Seth dress up as?
What does Gus dress up as?

What do you think?

Who is your favourite character from a book?
What is your favourite book?

Parents

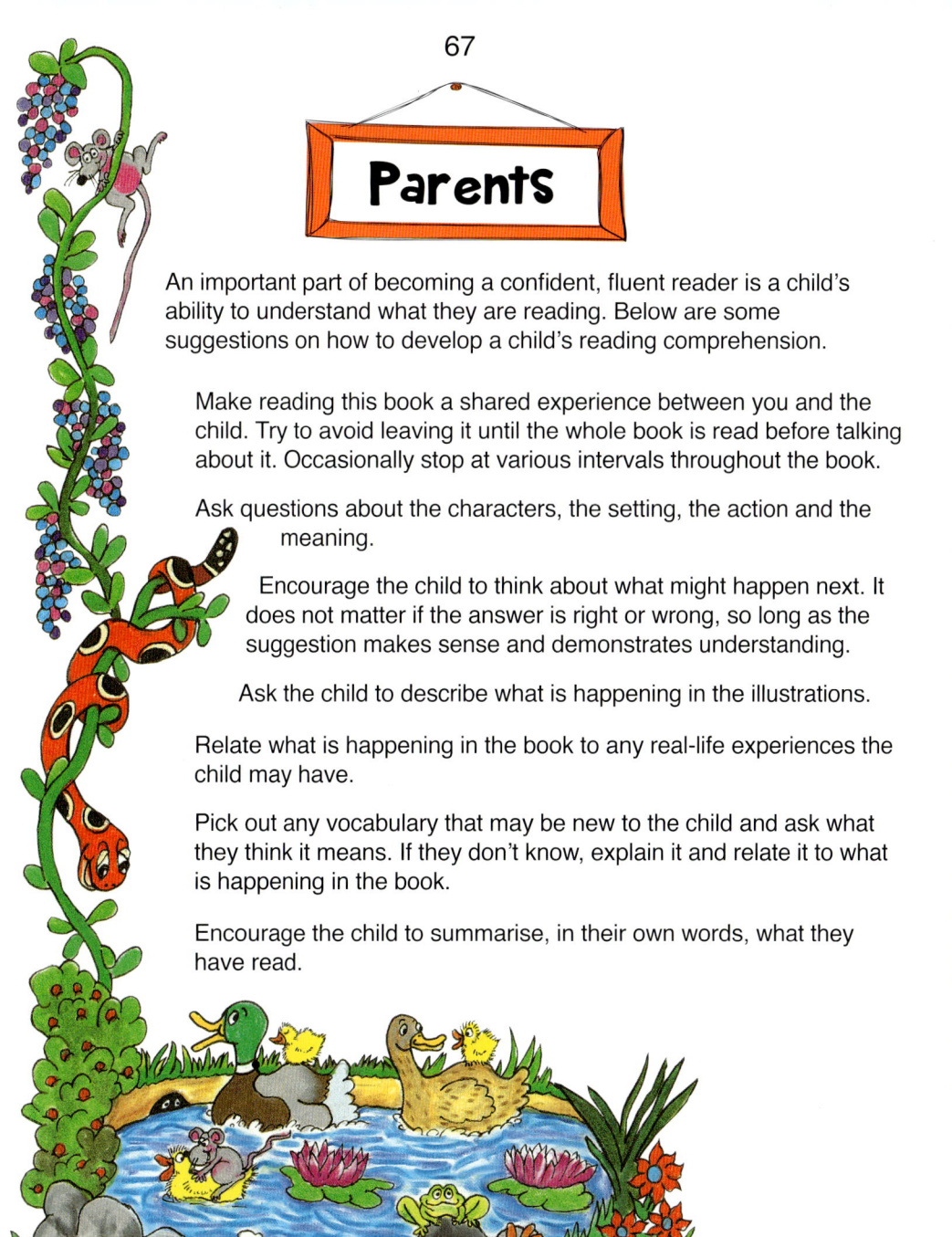

An important part of becoming a confident, fluent reader is a child's ability to understand what they are reading. Below are some suggestions on how to develop a child's reading comprehension.

Make reading this book a shared experience between you and the child. Try to avoid leaving it until the whole book is read before talking about it. Occasionally stop at various intervals throughout the book.

Ask questions about the characters, the setting, the action and the meaning.

Encourage the child to think about what might happen next. It does not matter if the answer is right or wrong, so long as the suggestion makes sense and demonstrates understanding.

Ask the child to describe what is happening in the illustrations.

Relate what is happening in the book to any real-life experiences the child may have.

Pick out any vocabulary that may be new to the child and ask what they think it means. If they don't know, explain it and relate it to what is happening in the book.

Encourage the child to summarise, in their own words, what they have read.

Book Review

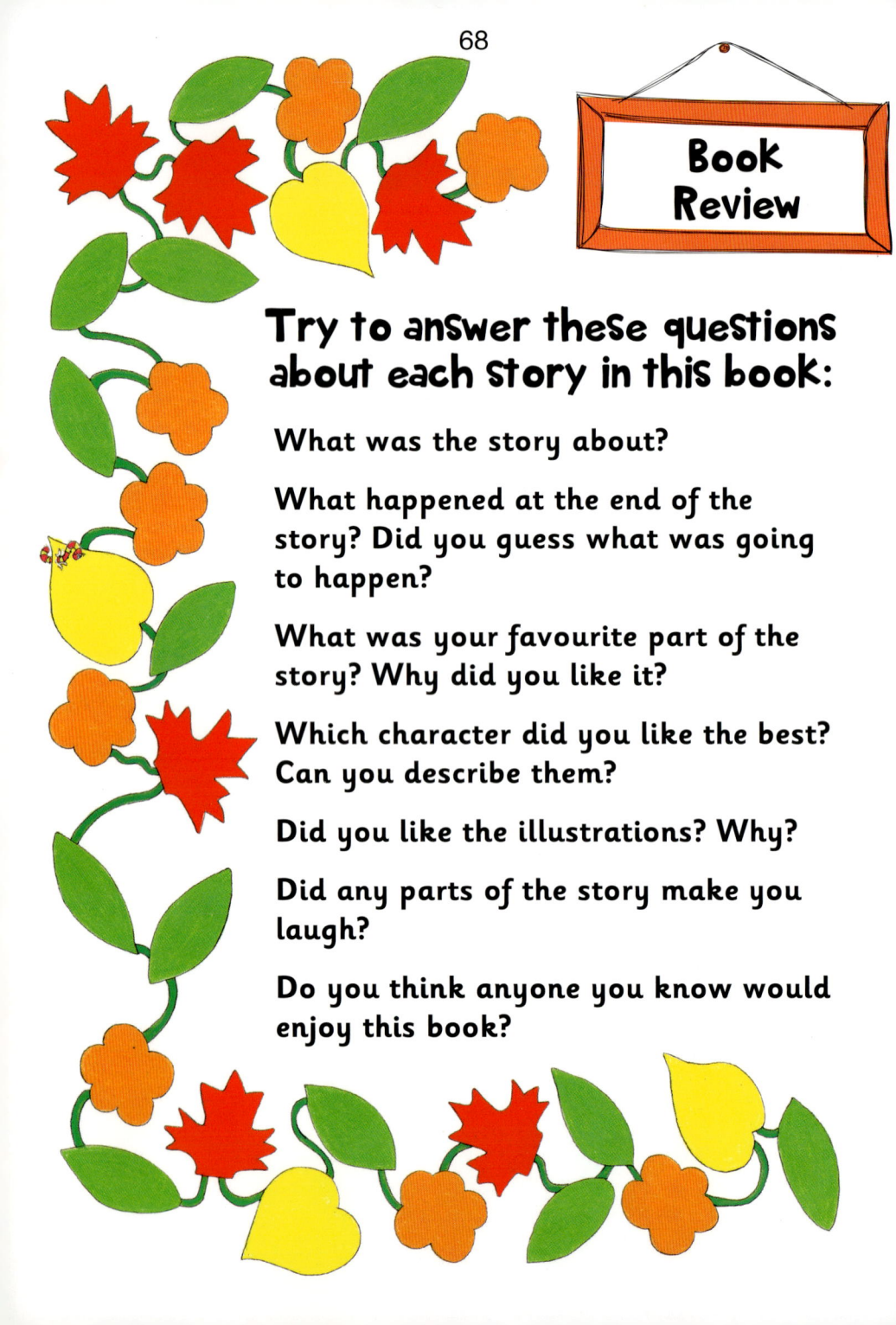

Try to answer these questions about each story in this book:

What was the story about?

What happened at the end of the story? Did you guess what was going to happen?

What was your favourite part of the story? Why did you like it?

Which character did you like the best? Can you describe them?

Did you like the illustrations? Why?

Did any parts of the story make you laugh?

Do you think anyone you know would enjoy this book?

Could you re-tell the story in your own words?

Has anything similar to this story ever happened to you?

Would you have liked this story to be shorter or longer?

Were there any parts of the story that you didn't like?

Have you read any stories that are similar to this one?

Would you enjoy reading this story again and would you recommend it to a friend?

Character Review

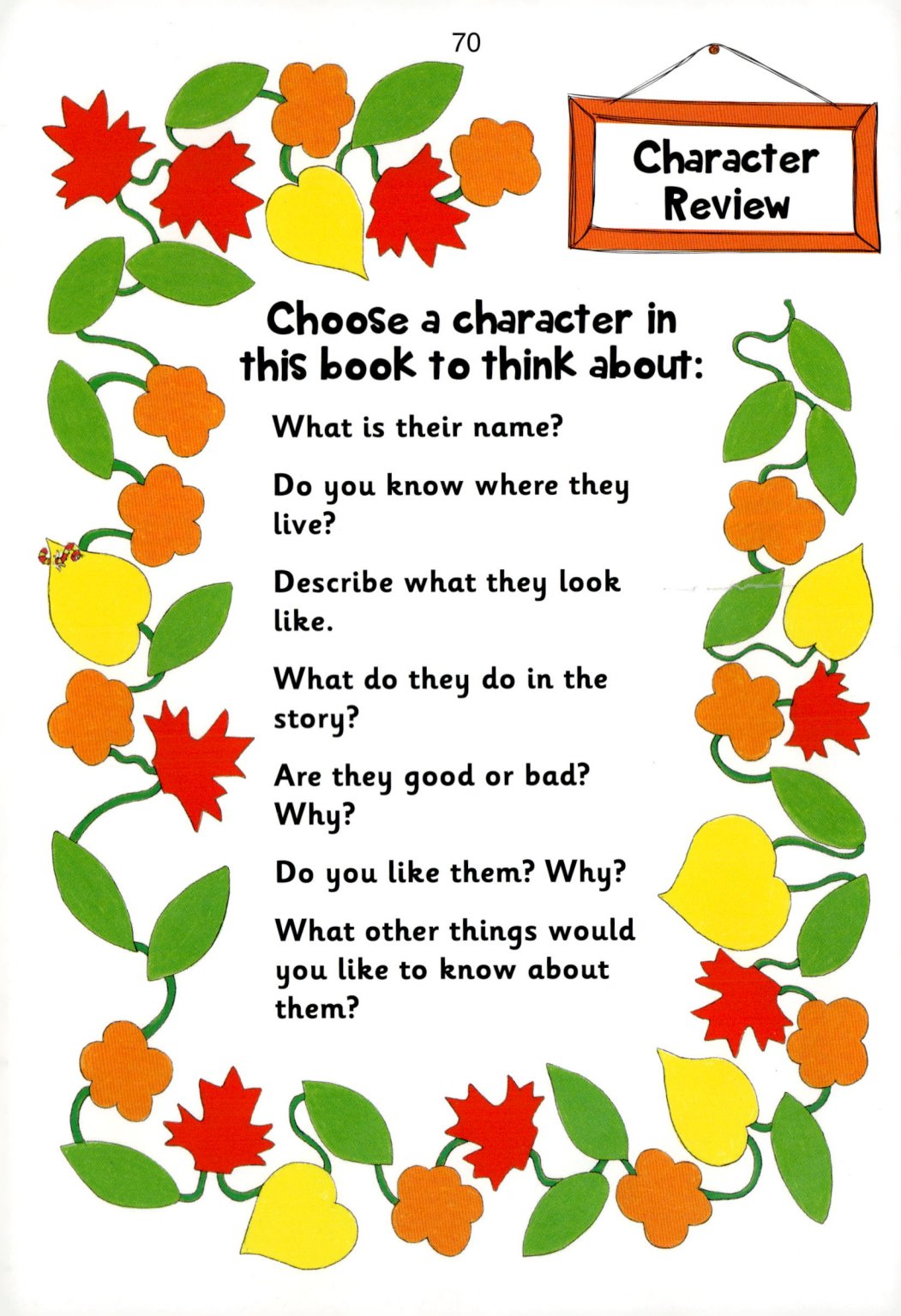

Choose a character in this book to think about:

What is their name?

Do you know where they live?

Describe what they look like.

What do they do in the story?

Are they good or bad? Why?

Do you like them? Why?

What other things would you like to know about them?